love, life & RECKLESSNESS
POEMS AND OTHER MUSINGS

A Creative Compilation By
ALLISON DENISE ARNETT

LOVE, LIFE, & RECKLESSNESS
Copyright © 2019 Allison Denise Arnett
All rights reserved.

This book or any portion thereof may not be reproduced or used in any manner whatsoever without the express written permission of the publisher except for the use of brief quotations in a book in review.

Cover & Interior Design by BrandItBeautifully™
www.branditbeautifully.com
www.loveliferecklessness.com

ISBN: 978-0-578-59328-9
Printed in the United States of America

DEDICATION

To your creative soul.
May you know her and be her... (or him).

TABLE OF CONTENTS

7	*Acknowledgments*
9	Creative Soul 1: Allison Denise
21	Creative Soul 2: Clarissa Pritchett
35	Creative Soul 3: Deborah Rivers Decoteau
47	Creative Soul 4: Keithra Morley
55	Creative Soul 5: Larkeia Matthews
63	Creative Soul 6: Love King
71	Creative Soul 7: Mz Mahoghany Reignz
83	Creative Soul 8: Patti Denise
93	Creative Soul 9: Srebrenica Lejla
103	Creative Soul 10: Takima Howze
115	*About the Authors*

ACKNOWLEDGEMENTS

Thank You God for making me in your image to be a creative being here on Earth and thank you to every lady who said yes to the call of sharing your creative offerings for this publication.

Love, Life, & Recklessness

Allison
DENISE

Love, Life, & Recklessness

She is Handpicked by God

Love, Life, & Recklessness

One

A

One second glance had me shook then a
One minute chat had me hooked then a
One hour embrace was the start of the
One day when you stole my heart and
One month compiled of us two fills my
One a.m. thoughts of you
...sleep don't come easy when you're not here

Allison Denise Arnett

Melodious

We both speak in

Song lyrics and serenades

Dancing together in a

Beautiful haze Our melody

Sparked by a long deep gaze

... O'MusicMan I have loved you for days

Allison Denise Arnett

When I

And when I look in his eyes

I see smiling at our grandkids' graduation

And when I fall in his embrace

I hold onto all the years of love to come

And when I hear his laugh

I listen for every happy anniversary we will speak

And when I kiss his lips...Well...

I fall in love all over again

...with his everything

Allison Denise Arnett

Romans 8:28

Sometimes the risks I take

Turn into the mistakes I make

I am better for the mistakes I make.

They teach me.

And grow me.

And sometimes

The wrong choices lead us to the right places.

After all

...all things work together for my good.

Allison Denise Arnett

The UnLovables

Some people didn't come to be loved.
They were sent to show us ourselves.
To help us grow.
And it is that in and of itself
...that makes them lovable.

Allison Denise Arnett

Sleep Tight

You lay here

Breathing

Comfortable enough to rest

Sleep easy baby

Meanwhile my heart is dancing to the rhythm of

And finding its relaxation in

Your ins and outs

Your rises and falls

I love it all man

...your white noise

Allison Denise Arnett

Destiny's Design

Mom: Singer/Cultural Dancer/Costume Designer

Dad: Guitarist/Singer/Songwriter

I...I am a child of art.

I speak in song lyrics.

I move in rhythm.

I see the world in color.

Music is my love.

Dance is my therapy.

I am Allison Denise

...and I must create.

Allison Denise Arnett

Blessings from the Lord

Early, On time, and Super Early
Inquisitive, Creative, and Bold
Kind, Caring, and Loving
All before eleven years old

Quiet, Talkative, Energetic
Gaming, Crafting, and Dance
Attentive, Spunky, and Feisty
Stealing hearts with a glance

To the untrained eye It looks like I gave you life
But in reality...
Every...Day
You. Give. Me. Life.
And I thank God for you
Describing you, I describe myself
...Children are reflections

Allison Denise Arnett

Clarissa PRITCHETT

Love, Life, & Recklessness

Love, Life, & Recklessness

She Grew from Concrete

Roses are meant to be beautiful,
Roses are meant to be wanted,
brighter and beyond what grief can hold,
But some roses are left as broken
glass on the sidewalk of life.
That rose you see glittering wasn't so shiny before,
deserted, ridiculed and
tossed away like unwanted seeds.

These leaves are light; a light that
Shines on her.
She grew from concrete; stronger than
every hardest struggle you may ever imagine.
The concrete was on the way side, heart side, and home side.
The concrete was the essence of her life,
harder than cracking a diamond.
The Rose that grew from Concrete
was she, do you know why some
roses have golden pendants?
They are a testimonial to the struggles
she went through and through.

How do you live when everything and everyone
that should matter wants you to leave?

Love, Life, & Recklessness

How do you become free when the world you live in is a prison?
She was just a native of that soil,
An existing flower under that concrete.

The concrete was decorated with different layers of coming from
Single parenthood, odds, personal struggles,
neglect, rejection, resentment, unhealthy love
And all other layers you can't imagine with words alone.
Nobody believed in her,
not even those she loved.
The world was a frame, only which she could see,
home was a fantasy, an unrealized happiness,
a dream chased without
any hope in sight.

She grew more and watching the moon,
counting the stars and taking the
Freshness of the sun hoping they will
all shine on her life that is a rose.
This year's gleam was the same every year.
You can't ignore your inner mind,
you can't say no to the true world you want,
no matter how dark.

She's A Creative Soul

She needed the love that would be all she need
But that was a crime,
They know she will only get hurt,
Broken and left with shapeless memories
Of all the hardest things in life.

All things comely and unneeded,
all roses come in fine pieces
But broken things are new in the morning,
Splashing newness when the night time is over.
This rose that grew concrete
Became the length of the world,
Changed, transformed
And reflecting newness.
This particular rose blossoms
other roses in the hearts of others,
hearts apart, hearts near, and hearts that will never be found.

That the image she lived reminiscing on
Will not be the fate of others,
Had she not been awake, that a beautiful
Rose light her deep sleep.
She slept, a rose did, so that
She can shine light on others to grow from concreate too.

Clarissa Pritchett

You Can Sit with Me

They didn't let you sit with them.
I know the feeling all to well.
Please allow me to remind you,
Never let people change you.
Just sit with only the ones that bring out the best in you;
the parts already sitting beneath the surface
waiting for the clouds of self-doubt to clear
and the real you to shine through like the sun.
You can sit with me,
I'll show you the potential
which hides from you
when you look in the mirror.
I'll show you the light
which radiates when you smile.
I'll look forward to the day
when you build your own table.
I'll still be around
mile after mile
reminding you that
billboard beauty
isn't a reality
it's an idea
a dream
sold

She's A Creative Soul

to those

who can't see

that beauty can't be

captured in an image

mirages can be painted every day

filled with color and life.

You can sit with me

and I'll show you

that beauty is shining bright through your crown.

Beauty can't be bought.

Remember drones are better left in the sky,

uniformed and unadorned

by life's battle scars.

The scar on your knee

the covered scars on your face,

beauty is in the eye of the beholder.

You can sit with me

and I'll show you

that your body isn't a prison of imperfection.

Your worth will never depend on

size, shape, and color.

Our bodies are not bookends

to be left on a shelf

collecting dust

waiting to be read.

They're instruments of celebration

Love, Life, & Recklessness

if you allow yourself the freedom
to feel alive in the skin your in
with no regrets or apologies.
No two stars are the same,
no one can shine bright like you.
I'll be here to remind and inspire you
to show you that the lies you've been told
about your self-worth simply aren't true.
Not every Queen gets the same crown
and every woman deserves to be uplifted
when they're down.
The gutter is no place for royalty Queen
so sit beside me at the table of life
as I cheer and clap for you to ascend.

Clarissa Pritchett

Loving Me in My Recklessness

God thank you for loving me
in my recklessness.

I was rolling dice
knowing you paid the price.
God thank you for loving me
in my recklessness.

You saw me at my worst
and forgave my mistakes.
God thank you for loving me
in my recklessness.

You made sure I landed on my feet
when I dove head first.
God thank you for loving me
in my recklessness.

I put myself in dangerous situations
and put my life in the hands of those that bruised me
God thank you for loving me
in my recklessness.

You drew the line in my life many times

Love, Life, & Recklessness

and I still found a way to cross it.
God thank you for loving me
in my recklessness.

You were by my side through thick and thin,
you never let me go.
God thank you for loving me
in my recklessness.

Those times I knew I should wake up to put you first
But kept choosing You as number two.
God thank you for loving me
in my recklessness.

You had a plan for my life that I couldn't see
and I kept walking blind in the dark knowing you are the light.
God thank you for loving me
in my recklessness

I can see now why you never left my side,
I'm loving the life you brought me out of and into.
God thank you for loving me
in my recklessness.

Clarissa Pritchett

She's A Creative Soul

The Apple of God's Eye

A battlefield, a smoky haze.
Her fathers suicide following her first young breath.
Surviving him, a fractured home and
her mother left with a daughter to raise alone.

Invisible walls became a prison.
Chained souls serving life in a small town.
Distant freedom dwelled within her vision.
She knew she could fly instead of being rooted.

They were blind. They could not see that
sometimes the apple falls far from the tree.
They told her. They Warned her. When she
didn't listen, they refused her.

They told her what she couldn't do and what
she couldn't be. Sometimes she was a little too
dark or a bit too light. They told her what to do,
and that they were the ones that truly knew, her
life would never turn out right.

Their words fell not on deaf ears but on a strong
mind unwilling to take as her own their
unrelenting fears. She knew that the weak live

their lives as a mossy stone never straying from
the dry desert they call home.

She knew that just as the clouds in the sky
dance in the spiral of freedom unshackled and
unencumbered by the chains of man, she too
would fly high, as whispers in her ear said, "you
can't" and her heart screamed, "I can!"

From the ashes of the battlefield, she fell farther away.
With faith, she brought the walls crashing down,
bursting free from the prison of her small town.
Knowing that imprisonment is within the mind,
she set out, her success to find.

The difficult path brought highs and lows, great
success and suffered blows. She climbed and
sometimes she fell, each step, her story to tell.
With every fall, she got up again.
Refusing to stop before reaching the top, she achieved by
being who she's always been.
The apple of God's eye.

Clarissa Pritchett

Deborah Rivers Decoteau

Love, Life, & Recklessness

Falling in Love

It was a normal day. I was still very young and innocent.
Living in my parents' home on the island of Trinidad.
At fifteen I did many fun things like playing in the streets with
my brothers, sisters, and the neighbor's children.
But my most favorite thing to do of all was going to the village
community center twice per week to learn to dance;
Not before completing my homework and chores of course.

This particular evening though, I didn't know, but my life would
change forever. My younger sisters and I took our usual
walk to the community center to meet our dance instructor,
Charlie. Once every so often, Charlie would bring different
dancers from his own village to help him. As I walked into the
community center eager to see, what Charlie had in store for
us... I saw him.

He was sitting outside the center on a bench with a guitar
under his arm. Dark, pink chapped lips, a huge afro, a casual
t-shirt and jeans. "Who was this?" I thought. He was reserved
and very different than the other helpers that came with
Charlie. He said "hello" to us as we passed by, and when he
smiled, I felt my heart flutter and skip a beat. A feeling I have
never felt before.

Love, Life, & Recklessness

During one of our rest periods he started strumming his guitar. Immediately all the young ladies gathered around him... Including me... I did not understand what I was feeling at the time, I was shy and nervous. All the while, not knowing that this young man was not just tall, dark, and handsome, he was also talented.

I will never forget that moment until the day I die.
The song... "Killing Me Softly" by Roberta Flack
His gaze was on me the whole time he sang
At the end, he blinked at ME! Or as we say in Trinidad he gave me a "sweet eye" meaning... "I see you." At that point I melted.

His name? Franklin
My heart? Falling in Love
My Life? Forever Changed

Deborah Rivers DeCoteau

Let's Just Kiss and Say Goodbye

Seventeen. Experiencing love for the first time and making plans. Mommy was a housewife and Daddy worked in the oil business. Work had Daddy traveling back and forth from Trinidad to the Virgin Islands almost always. My siblings and I traveled with him sometimes too during summer when school was out. Life was great!

One day Mommy told us that Daddy would be going far away to work in America. A place called Texas where there was a lot of work for him. Daddy was gone a long while and in the mean time, my beloved and I continued to see each other in secret; despite my parents' disapproval. I was in love for Pete's sake!

When Daddy finally returned home from Texas after about a year, we were happy to see him. Not so happy to hear what he was planning. During his stay in Texas, he'd bought a house and apparently we were all moving to Texas to live.

"Texas!" I said, "The land with horses and cowboys!" He laughed. I was dismayed. I did not want to leave Trinidad and I sure didn't want to leave my beloved. I was so devastated. I begged not to go. I wanted to stay in Trinidad, live with my grandmother, finish school, then marry my beloved. "No!" My parents answer was a resounding NO! And I was most assuredly moving to the land of cowboys.

I cried and my beloved comforted me.
"Let's just run away and get married!" I said. "I don't want you to forget about me!"

Time drew near and our visits become more difficult to pull off. Daddy found out and was keeping an eye on his babygirl. I cried myself to sleep almost every night. My beloved, being the type of man he was, treated me like I was the only woman in the world. I never had to second-guess him and he gave me unconditional love. He would tell me, "Obey your parents. I could never forget about you. We will meet again soon and all our plans would become a reality."

The most requested song on the radio during that time was by the Manhattans..."Let's Just Kiss and Say Goodbye" And the night before I left Trinidad that is exactly what we did. We just kissed and said goodbye.

Young love
Torn apart
Beating hearts
Forever intertwined

Deborah Rivers DeCoteau

The House on the Hill

The first time I saw you it was love at first sight
Your smile, your lips, your style
I wanted to know more about you but I was nervous and shy
You sang to me and let me know you were feeling it too
I wanted to know your name, where you lived, were you single.
However, I was shy and nervous, and not ready to mingle
I wanted to laugh with you instead of laughing with them
Then you spoke and asked my name and told me you were Franklin

Franklin the man who'd change my life forever
Visiting my parents home to find out whether or not you could date me
Of course my parents said no because I was still not quite old enough to date... but it was too late
I was already in love
With the dark skinned young fella from the house on the hill.

I saw you as my husband; father of my future children
Some time with you at the house on the hill I went to spend
You invited me in and I accepted
Not really sure what was being expected
I sat on the sofa, you sat next to me
I could feel my heartbeat, my whole body going crazy

Love, Life, & Recklessness

"What is this I am feeling?" Was repeating in my head
"Am I ready for this? Are we going to bed?"

Somehow I felt safe but still nervous you know?
To help calm my nerves you offered me some H2O
You led me into your bedroom after taking my hand
Once again, there was that feeling I did not understand

I remember you asking if I'm scared, I said "yes."
The kiss you then offered to help quiet my fears was the best
At the edge of the bed your soft hands warm my face
The whole world disappeared and I was feeling great!

I felt your tongue in my mouth
My head gently elevated, resting in the palm of your hands,
My eyes closed, my legs became weak as I kissed you back and
At that moment, all my fears disappeared and curiosity set in
Alone with you , my beloved, at the house on the hill

You gently laid me on the bed and began to undress me
You touched my breast and caressed them ever so gently
My breathing got louder and louder I was ready to feel
What it would be like to
Take our love another step at the house on the hill

You took off your clothes and I saw it for the first time

She's A Creative Soul

I reached out and touched what was rightfully mines
You proceeded to enter me as our kiss grew more intense
All was going well until that moment when
I cried out for you to stop on the house on the hill

You immediately stopped and asked what was the matter
I told you it hurt
You the apologized telling me that you'd rather not cause me
any pain and that it was ok
And a silence took over the house on the hill that day

We quietly got dressed and you led me to the half opened
bedroom window overlooking the neighborhood
You put your arms around me and we both stared speechless
at the beautiful green scenery as we stood

Silenced was broken when you offered to take me home
"I will wait til you're ready", you said in a caring tone
We proceeded to leave, still in love yet unfulfilled
On our first of many a splendid days at
the the house on the hill

Deborah Rivers DeCoteau

Love, Life, & Recklessness

Keithra MORLEY

Love, Life, & Recklessness

Love, Life, & Recklessness

She's A Creative Soul

Lose to Win

I once had to let go of
the only thing I'd known for the past 14 years
It hurt so much to hang on
I was slowly dying inside
Felt like I was drinking poison
and the cure was letting go
It wasn't until I walked away from the very person I loved
and discovered who I should have been loving in the first place
Myself

Keithra Morley

Let Go

I had to leave in order to receive.

Sometimes we are the ones blocking our own blessings.

Letting go isn't easy

But we need to

In order to make room for what God has in store for us.

Let go.

Keithra Morley

Forgiveness is for Me

I once thought by hating my enemy I was winning;
I mean I'd wish so many hurtful things would happen to them.
When I saw them a rage and anger would boil up inside of me,
To the point where I lashed out and threw tantrums.
It wasn't until I had gotten sick
And the doctors couldn't find what was wrong,
It was then I realized
I had been drinking poison called

Unforgiveness.

Keithra Morley

Love, Life, & Recklessness

Larkeia
MATTHEWS

Love, Life, & Recklessness

She is an Overcomer

Love, Life, & Recklessness

Alive

I want to feel alive,
Not just heart beating and breathing but pulsating with vision and drive.
The people I help heal or teaching someone to build, in serving my purpose anothers purpose will be revealed.
Not waisting my life means I value my time creating legacies that will live on line after line.
I crave the feeling I get when I see a baby smile .
The energy it gives makes my heart run wild.
This is why I dare , I strive, I need to feel alive,
Not just heart beating and breathing but ensuring, my legacy survives.
So I chase passionate moments and enduring embraces.
I delight in the possibility I see on young dreamers faces.
A 401K and mundane day to day , no way.
I would rather chase the feeling of catching a bouquet.
Alive is those moments that you stop playing small,
throw caution to the wind like you're not afraid to fall.
Its stepping out your comfort zone and into a new space,
its knowing life is too full of possibility to keep playing it safe.
You've embraced it when you no longer survive , you thrive,
Cause It's the moments in between your heart beating and breathing that makes you Alive!

Larkeia Matthews

Emerge

As I look over my life, what do I see
I see Good and, both greatness and complacency.
Of darkness and light I have seen both sides,
Somehow the laughs and smiles were overlooked because of the cries.
Because of the hurt I had built up such disdain,
I was showing love and still receiving pain.
so I hid from love to see no hurt, I would not chance or dare where disappoints could lurk,
This wall was formed to defend me, but it left my heart cold and rather empty.
It meant that I couldn't reach that high, couldn't amount to much, couldn't look love in the eye,
But What kind of life would this be,
If I let the worst get the best of me!
All of a sudden, like Immediately, I became FED UP with mediocrity!
That path had led me to the verge, that the only thing left to do was to Emerge!
Emerge from disbelief that FALSE truths have founded,
Emerge from fear that had my dreams surrounding,
Emerge from bitterness that holds my heart captive, releasing

anger, and regret and start being proactive.
Emerge from limiting beliefs because they mean me no good,
less focus on what I can't and more on what I COULD!
Yes I can, says a voice within.
YOU are a Powerful force is what I hear again and again.
You can have what you say, just learn to create.
You've been given the pen so, go, design your fate!

Larkeia Matthews

Restore

I was given a lesson on how to let my heart breathe
I was holding it so tightly giving it no space to grieve.
Resentment filled my heart cause it seemed that love had let me down, but was it me that missed the clues and the warnings all around.
How can I be hurt that my delusion didn't last, there was a time allotted for us, and that time we pushed past.
Trying time and time again to do the same wrong thing, is a misuse of persistence more likened to a fiend.
The same repetition with different expectations,
Gives anybody an insane reputation.
Something had to change and why shouldn't it be me.
I am the Empress, Master, and Orator of my own
Destiny. Seasons can change depending on our awareness,
Your openness to change, dedication and preparedness.
No situation is out of your control,
The power lies within just believe, Embrace and Behold.

Larkeia Matthews

Love, Life, & Recklessness

Her beauty is more than Skin deep

Love, Life, & Recklessness

Beloved

Beloved, why do you feel so blue?
Tell me who it was, that hurt you.
Beloved, why do you feel like you have to stay?
It's time to get away.

All the things you've done for him
He don't appreciate
Instead of him just loving you,
 he makes you think, it's you that he hates.
Don't wallow in his self-pity,
cause there's plenty of people who love you.

Beloved, I beg of you to come and go with me.
Beloved, I hate to see you in such misery.
Beloved why do you think that you have to stay?
It's time to get Away.

Love King

And Still I Rise

I Rise above the clouds in the sky.
I Rise while life is trying to weigh me down.
Despite my frustration,
I Rise to the occasion because of this deep dedication I have inside.
I Rise above the voice that tries to drop me down below into the darkest places of my mind.
I Rise when life is stretching me wider than the ocean's surface.
I Rise above the pain, above the tears, above the rejection I fear the most.
I've been knocked down, but I rise to the opportunity to get back up again.
I've been hated and despised and still I rise with love.

Love King

In These Streets

I ran into that Baltic Avenue cat named Misery, I used to love me some him
He loved my company until I stopped being an employee and stretched my mind to become the CEO.
He left me.
Spilled milk is not enough for me to cry over, I can't take that chance.
I will take my get out a jail free card, and park my free will to let Jesus take the wheel.
I been blessed to pass go and collect another $200
Whew!! I dodged a bullet
I haven't landed on boardwalk yet but I'm on my way
before I could live in wealth and luxury
I had to walk in these streets of my past to clean out the rotten gutters.

Love King

Opposites Attract

She's present

But His attention is at a deficit

He's bankrupt

She needs attention

He can't pay it.

She is another man's treasure.

She Trusted

He lied

She invested

He insufficient funded

She is the Lottery… He didn't win!!

She Tried

He didn't

She stayed

He left (the grass is greener)

He's back (fake green grass)

She's gone!!

Love King

Mz Mahoghany
REIGNZ

Love, Life, & Recklessness

She is Sweet & Talented

Love, Life, & Recklessness

She's A Creative Soul

A Daisy Destined To Become A Rose

For now my words are only on this page, but soon my words will be on many pages-the world is my stage; read worldwide by countless numbers that flow like rivers, or a lyricist's flowing effortlessly…words, so beautiful so free, Majestic and distinctive- Dreams become memories like "remember that time?!" lol- and even remind myself of the time when I could only cry and shake the reality of a photogenic memory- Developing too vividly from the efficiencies they occupy in the prison cells of my mind…

Sometimes in order to get a positive to expose you need a negative-Like a Polaroid-that speaks of many people's story… They say a picture speaks a thousand words…so my words must be a gallery of twisted lines and colorful blends that are timeless…which means there is no end

Not breaking records, but setting records like grandma used to do my hair on a Saturday night for church the next morning

Words so fire they crackle and sizzle with blue magic as if they were on a hot comb sliding through your head

Flow so wet my roots begin to show

I'm just a dope filled daisy determined to prove that the concrete from which I grew- Never had the ability to stunt my evolution into a dynamic rose

Mz Mahoghany Reignz

My Personal Belongings

Like an addict looking for his next high…you came in to
me, with determination in your eyes that was so fierce and
piercing…No wonder I
Fell prey to your demands, unable or even willing – to come
to my God-given senses to take a stand and say one two letter
word… NO!
I'm not that weak person you had created so long ago; Full of
low self-esteem unable to let the nothingness you gave me go
I want my stuff back
I mean I want everything you stole
And I'm taking it back by the violent force I should have used
so many times before
This is what you helped to create, so please don't make the
terrible mistake of trying to fight me for what's mine, because
you will surely lose
Like a string of fine pearls ripped from my neck, you tore my
confidence down with every pull of my emotions as my tears
fell to the floor one at a time
Soal
King the flood like a slow and steady summer rain
How was I ever able to look at your face and see anything
except a reflection of my pain
I want my stuff back! That's what my stilettos echo with every
step I take to freedom your controversial prison of lust you

She's A Creative Soul

masked for so long as love

Give me back my stuff!

I'm gonna need you to release my creativity, because it's not even mine

It belongs to God and was presented to me as a gift to use for His glory and edification

Unchain my heart and take the Kung Fu grip off my common sense, because I need to use them both again, along with my compassion that was buried so deep within

It took Jesus to reach down deep into the very abyss you constructed for my destruction and Jesus so gracefully brought it back to the surface of my mind

See I came back to get my stuff and this time I'm for real this is not a test of the emergency broadcast system

This my dear is not a drill! GIVE ME BACK MY STUFF!!!!!!!

Mz Mahoghany Reignz

Mz Mahoghany Reignz

I took some clouds in my life to create this side of me…Last name reignz first name Mahoghany
Passion and pain living life without much gain, over whelmed by the sheer idea of not surviving in this world, losing the game
Mahoghany reignz
I was born from a rainbow of colorful truths and dark colored lies
I am the personification of Stephanie Michelle's determination to prosper and survive
You may not know me, until now neither did she, but now Im here and I hold the lock to her heart and only God has the key
Mz Mahoghany Reignz is what you need to call me
See, Mz Mahoghany was shaped by events that made me strong, although at the time I thought I would die
But like a phoenix from the ashes I rise
Hence giving birth to my more confident and sassy side
The voice of my confidence that used to fade in the distant abyss of my uninvited shame
Mz Mahoghany Reignz
I am the icing on the cake too real to be fake
I am the ideal alter ego that never takes a back seat
A diva in the highest regard
Sometimes soft sometimes hard
Ready to make sure we will remain

Glad to meet your acquaintance
IM MZ MAHAGHANY REIGNZ

Mz Mahoghany Reignz

Unconscious Low Self-esteem

She never realized her own unique beauty; For she was so focused on her flaws
Arising from the ashes like a majestic phoenix-seemingly without effort- Not taking notice at all of her charm
Drawing attention like a moth to a flame that burns; but does not consume
If only she knew the power of her beauty
If only she could harness the unbridled passion that rests in the windows to her very soul
If only she tapped into her confidence as if it were the fountain of youth and drank from it until she was inebriated with love for herself
OOOOH How wondrous
How wondrously in awe would she be of her own natural beauty-If she allowed peace to be food to her malnourished soul
How magnificent would she feel if she could only devour her own self-loathing and replace it with unspeakable joy
She would flourish in her purpose and experience a mighty morphing of her perspective
She could marvel in the fact of being a designer's original
A timeless masterpiece that is valued beyond monetary measures
Priceless to say the least, she would forever increase in value

She's A Creative Soul

All because she finally did realize her flaws contribute to her own unique beauty
And gained the confidence that her stony ground could not and did not destroy her seed
It served as the venue to show the world her tenacity, strength and ability to still reach the sun

Mz Mahoghany Reignz

Love, Life, & Recklessness

Patti
DENISE

Love, Life, & Recklessness

Love, Life, & Recklessness

Love Is, Was, Remains...

Surviving the Clash of the Titans as we attempted to merge our core beliefs regarding faith, family, friends, fitness, food, finances, future. music, sex and everything! The frequent Tug-of-War which stemmed from not asking the right questions nor giving heed to intuition that screamed for us to slow down. We wrestled to maintain control, you know, the kind we had when we were single. Which one of us would acquiesce to the other, I mean, do we have to?

Both of us in desperate need to repair the other as we overlook our own brokenness. It was easier to observe the speck in the eye of my Lover than to deal with the log protruding from the corner of my left eye. With limited vision I approached with scalpel in hand ready to cut away what I perceived as imperfections while he too with his chisel awkwardly pounded at my flesh to bring out what he envisioned as the perfect woman.

Oh, the absurdity of it all! Is it possible that such a love would stand the test of time? We believed it could and with hands, heads and hearts entwined we knelt before our creator on a regular and whispered the promises of our eternal vows to always love each other. In moments of passion we were blameless and spotless and limitless until the crescendo drained us of selfishness, and we became one. Our only desire was to please each other and nothing or no one else mattered. The dialogue repeatedly ended with each one responding to the other "I want whatever you want."

Night would turn into day and day to night and the harmony was effortless as we included our thanks to God in our chorus of how sweet it is to be loved by you. Hours of IP Man, Shaolin Monks and Kung Fu. Meals prepared and brought to bed as we shared. Date nights with movies and dinners for two. Showed up with Heineken in my handbag just for you. Smile. When did the tides turn? When did the implosion begin? What force was so diabolical and when did it sneak in? Unaware of its power we toyed with disaster until. I cannot speak for the other, but I vowed to discover what it was about me that needed to change. The gift I received as my exit strategy was to survive this dilemma without blame. It is mature to admit when you realize that you are contributing to the suffering of another soul and be strong enough to let go. After all, "a bird could love a fish...but where would they live?" (Joseph Stein) Life goes on and a Love like that... Is, Was and Remains.

Patti Denise Henry

Life is a Gift

Years ago I listened in on a conversation and one of the individuals stated "As soon as I began
to understand what life was all about, it was time for me to go." He continued sharing of his terminal
diagnosis and although I was there to provide spiritual support I began breathing heavily as I found
myself in a private panic. Several thoughts raced through my mind which led me to ask myself the
following questions: What is life? What is my life? Am I living or barely existing? Existential concerns
bombarded my psyche. Overhearing that conversation was truly a gift to me that day. I then, with a
quiet persistence accompanied by a passionate resolve began to live on purpose and without apologies.
I learned that life ebbs and flows and is packed with both mountaintop and valley experiences. I
learned that you cannot truly say that you have had a bad day until all your days were in. I learned not
take anyone or anything for granted... Life is a journey we make through this parentheticals space we
refer to as "time" We experience birth, childhood, awkwardness, we celebrate milestones such as
graduation, marriage and various rites of passage. Our characters become defined. Like sands through

the hourglass is all of this really the best days of our lives?
Unfortunately, most of us never understand
why or what life is all about. I've learned to appreciate my life
by serving the dying. I have experienced
through observation the pain of regret that many people face
when they realize that their life is now
threatened by a terminal condition. The precious trusted
moments ignited my passion to live I wanted
to taste it all. To be vulnerable. To take chances. I began to
intentionally live and to breathe.

Patti Denise Henry

My First Yes

Hearts racing….

Mine busting out my chest

His in alignment

This moment is no jest

Awkward fingers doing the most

Penetrating layers

Of monsters and ghost

Ghosts of abusers past

Monsters are the ones still present.

I tremble.

Confused and afflicted

Do I want to do this?

Is the yes in my head

My own? Do I do this?

This thing that I'm feeling

It's not like before

My choice, my voice

Yes… Yes

You have permission to explore

Patti Denise Henry

Srebrenica
LEJLA

Love, Life, & Recklessness

She lives in full Color

Love, Life, & Recklessness

The Strong Ones

Sometimes we don't realize our strength, until after the storm. We look back in awe of our perseverance, our faith, the commitments that we've made to ourselves. We never thought we'd make it to today. This beautiful day.

Yet still we stand. Stronger than ever.

To the person who seems to have it all together, being the support to others, and seemingly crushing goals, it is normal to have moments of not being the one.

So I say this:

Be mindful of the strong ones around you. They are more vulnerable than you think. Cry more than you know. Struggle more than you know.

Just because they don't show these things, doesn't mean to turn a blind eye to what's unseen.

Be mindful of the strong ones.
Their battles are much more challenging than you could imagine.

Be mindful of the strong ones.
You may see their confidence and smile, but you have no idea of the struggles they deal.

Be mindful. Be kind. Simply smile. Speak to that person walking by.
It may be a stranger or it might be your own relatives.
Extend that smallest acknowledgment, something so subtle.
The gentle reminder,
They are not alone.

Srebrenica Lejla

The (un)Usual Relationship

We seldom talk about the mental and psychological abuse women (and men) go through when they are in said abusive relationships. It took a whole two years after I let go to realize the long-term effects a psychologically abusive relationship had on me.

At first, I was in denial because my favorite line was "He has never put his hands on me, therefore I wasn't abused". Sounds familiar? According to the 2019 National Coalition Against Domestic Violence (NCADV), "48.4% of women and 48.8% of men have experienced at least one psychologically aggressive behavior by an intimate partner, while 7 out of 10 psychologically abused women display symptoms of PTSD and/or depression".

I was extremely insecure while people pleasing became a burden mentally, spiritually, and financially. It was like I cut myself off from loving me. Truth is, you can't love someone so much that you devalue yourself in the end. I did that for two years. Lost myself trying to love and build someone else.

Being that young, baby 20-something who was so naive of wanting to be loyal to someone who's narcissistic ways almost shattered me.

Nothing I did was right. I always asked for approval with the pretense that it still wouldn't meet his standards. Having the fear that if you did not please him, he would see no value in you. I stayed hopeless, depressed, and on edge all the time. I'm surprised I passed my college classes.

Eventually, I gained the courage to let go and simply walk away. I let go of pouring into someone who is not being reciprocal. I let go of feeling inferior, like I wasn't enough. I let go of being mentally enslaved by someone who told me "No one will ever want to be with you".

For a while I was afraid of commitment, placing this huge wall to protect myself from being let down again. Even with guys I did date, something always triggered me and I immediately withdrew myself. It was a vicious cycle, I soon got tired of and had to really learn how to love myself first. Be unapologetically selfish.

Self-love is the best love. Self-love always come first. Self-love is invigorating, refreshing. Self-love allows us to create healthy boundaries.

If you're ever in doubt. Choose you first.
Srebrenica Lejla

Reference: https://www.speakcdn.com/assets/2497/domestic_violence_and_psychological_abuse_ncadv.pdf

Platonic Relationships

Often difficult to find, but once you come across one it is one of the best relationships. Platonic relationships have a natural way of bringing out the best in you.

Your communication skills heighten, turning into a mutual mentorship.

Boundaries are clearly defined and respected, you learn discipline.

The ability for a man and a woman having a strictly non-physical relationship. Like legit.

This is not friends with benefits!

No sex. None. Zilch. Nada.

There is no expectations set, that causes trouble if you do.

Can this be difficult? Possibly.

Can you retract and move a physical relationship to platonic?

Idk, if you attempt this and you're successful, lemme know.

I've seen relationships go from physical to non-physical. Shit happens. You lose interest, physically.

And that's okay.

Platonic relationships matter and… are necessary.

Srebrenica Lejla

Takima
HOWZE

Love, Life, & Recklessness

Love, Life, & Recklessness

Selfish

I don't want to share myself with nobody
Who can't handle my quick lip and chaos
Who knows all the answers to a complex me that I don't even understand
I don't want to share myself,
I'm selfish
Because who truly knows me and my thoughts when I'm alone behind closed walls and dreams
Thinking of million dollar hopes and nightmares that disguise themselves as dreams,
I'm Selfish and You Can't Handle Me
You think you know me but you've met my twin, the me that I want you to see and you've gotten so acquainted
You don't know me but you think you own me, I'm selfish with me, and you can never have me
I let you think you have right if passage to the core of my being
You've just undercut the surface and think you've found layers
Please I'm Selfish
You will never know me
I'm still on that journey, one you will never reach before me.

Takima Howze

It Gets Lonely

Some people won't tell the truth.
Walking around proud, smiling, happy to please all of you. But I can no longer play a facade, I needs to tell the truth before it destroys me inside,
I get lonely being me.
Alone with my thoughts replaying every moment I could have made a better, different choice.
It gets lonely being me.
Thinking upon thoughts day after day, pondering how my life could have went another way,
Yeah it gets lonely being me.
Wishing I had someone I could cry to, to tell all my secrets and fears too.
Yes, I have God, yes it's true, it's those lonely moments I want someBody there too,
See I told you I would tell the truth.
It's gets lonely being me. Running around enjoying purpose but who is there to ride with me.
No one at night to laugh and be excited when I want to share stories.
I thought I had someone but that was a lie, they don't know it but all they've ever done was make me cry. Second guess my life, my choices and who I am,
Controlling every aspect of my emotions just plain spent.

She's A Creative Soul

Crazy right? But that's my truth, and it would do you good to tell the truth too.

It's gets lonely being me. All by myself, with my baby. Praying to God to add another addition to our family.

She deserves more than I can provide and the truth of that tears me apart inside. I don't want her to feel the emptiness I feel. To want to fill those places with people and things and never be fulfilled.

I don't want her to be like me. Constantly questioning her identity she can't be lonely.

That's my True Story,

It gets lonely being me.

Takima Howze

Love, Life, & Recklessness

Beneath My Skin

Sometimes I wonder what beneath my skin,
The very depth within,
Through every crevice and cellular structured strand of hair
I think about
What is it that is under there?

I investigated the probabilities and soon discovered, the very essence
Of the shell that's on display
Some people say,
They see my glow, I not flashy or glossy,
I'm
Just reassured, you know
I know who I am and to whom I belong
And I am far to worthy to be a tag along

You see beneath this skin is all that I am
Full of majesty and honor by my master's hand
The precious blood that pours through my veins

Beneath My Skin,
I am destined to WIN

Takima Howze

Ode To You: As Me

I didn't see you coming nor did I expect you to be
So Me

I like your style and glow, you make me smile
You caught me by surprise

Everything about you is effortless even when you struggle
And so I am intrigued by you

How did you become so vibrant and fearless?
That's not me, or had it always been?

I admire you! Your tenacious spirit that flows and desires
To be FREE, indeed you are me

I am somewhat jealous of you, how you love so carelessly even
When people misTake, you, I wanna be like you

Some people say you favor me,
I say, you are God favor birthed in me

Indeed, you are a reflection of me, all of the me
I didn't believe I could see

Thank you for choosing to be an extension of me
The best parts of me, are you

Ode to You as Me

Takima Howze

Relinquish

It All
The power you believe you have to consume
To be on top

Of what?
You're not a god or Him who sits on high, come down
Can't you see your drunken ways of stupor
You are not the master of your destiny on your way to destruction!

See yourself...
Imagine the wind and waves of life crashing inside you
You're taken for a ride but you have not drowned
Relinquish all thought of believing it is you

Keeping you about the waters that trouble you,
You're not alone.
It's okay to give away the burdens you carry
You are not Mary you had the called bear the necessity of bringing His highness to all

Relinquish!

This is your call to lay it all down and decide to take up the lightwork

Accept your place

Peace in the value that puts back together all the Pieces that were you

Its Time

Relinquish

Takima Howze

About the AUTHORS

Love, Life, & Recklessness

Allison Arnett

Allison Denise is a Best-Selling Author, International Speaker, and Award-Winning Graphic Designer of beautiful boss brands and books. A servant leader at heart and an eclectic, creative soul, she seeks to help others free their creativity while transforming lives. An avid advocate of Self-Acceptance and Spiritual Empowerment it is her desire that every woman find the power in their voice and the beauty in their story. She currently resides in Houston, Texas with her three children.

Learn more about Allison Denise at
www.BrandItBeautifully.com
Social Media: @imallisondenise

Clarissa Pritchett

Clarissa Pritchett, M.P.H, is an Integrative Nutrition Health and Life Coach, Empowerment Speaker, Author, Entrepreneur, and Army Medical Service Corps Officer. Clarissa is a wife and mom to 3 beautiful boys. Clarissa is passionate about health and wellness and has served numerous clients over the past 17 years in the health and medical field. She has a Bachelors degree in Health Education, a Masters Degree in Public Health Nutrition and numerous certifications in the fitness and nutrition field. She is the founder of Healthy Family Kitchen and provides women/families with nutrition programs and strong faith fueled life recipes for life. Clarissa is also the founder of Empire Posh Queens and mentors women to start home businesses while promoting Sisterhood, Self-Care, and Service to those in need. She loves to encircle and uplift women to live healthy lives. She has written over 15 recipe E-books including health and wellness programs. She is a sought out Speaker and Resilience Instructor for the military, wellness companies, and local churches to share her story of overcoming health/life challenges and to motivate women with their health and life goals. Clarissa is a short, sweet, and spicy mixed salad sistah that keeps it real, raw and organic about how she overcame many health challenges and body issues. Overall, her favorite things in life are Jesus, family, friends, cooking and eating food, especially tacos, chocolate, and donuts with sprinkles!

You can find more information about Clarissa at: www.ClarissaPritchett.com and treat yourself to some healthy self-care at www.EmpirePoshQueen.com

Deborah Rivers DeCoteau

Originally from the island of Trinidad and Tobago, Deborah Rivers Decoteau relocated to Houston Texas her family in the mid 1970's. It is a known fact that wherever Trinidadians go, they transplant their carnival culture. Carnival and its traditions consist of the celebration of life, death, love and freedom portrayed in music, dance, song and beautifully decorated elaborate costumes. Being a Trinidadian at heart, Deborah had to get involved and dedicated her life to bringing awareness to her culture. Her journey: Founder and choreographer of LaTropical Dancers formerly known as Socalystics, sang her way into the annual Soca/Calypso Competition and won, designed carnival costumes and participated in the annual Parade of the Bands each year. She loves being from the Caribbean, her family, and GOD who will forever be part of her journey.

Keitha Morley

Keithra Morley is an inspirational powerhouse who loves God and shares His love wherever she goes. Her love for writing began when God saved her soul and changed her life. She penned her first book, Confessions of a Woman Saved by Grace in 2014. In addition to her book, she put her heart and soul into Confessions Uncensored, an original program that allows women to share their stories in a safe place, heal through writing, and share their stories with the world. Keithra has been a creative visionary for nearly 10 years. Keithra is from the beautiful island of the Bahamas. She enjoys spending time with her three beautiful children, Ahmad, Tajhanae and Tajhanique. She loves to sing, dance, mime, and read. Keithra loves chic and modest fashion and shopping. Kloset Konfessions was birthed as an extension to Confessions Uncensored. This chic and inspirational apparel line is for the woman who knows that grace is the one thing that makes life worth living. Keithra hopes that Kloset Konfessions will allow women around the world to become a walking announcement of God's message of love and grace.

Larkeia Matthews

Larkeia Keyonna Matthews, CEO/ Founder of national Empowerment coaching and training business called H.E.R Legacy in HEELS. Larkeia started her professional education in Psychology at Victory University in Memphis, TN while obtaining state licensing in Real Estate Sales. After the hearing loss of her oldest son Larkeia was faced with a setback in her education. She decided to be totally available to her son's recovery all the while devising a strategy to bounce back and create a new path to her goals. Before deciding to officially launch H.E.R Legacy, Larkeia informally educated herself for 4 years in areas of personal growth and development, Spirituality, universal laws, and the art of Speaking and coaching. She joined virtual campuses and programs and semiars of some of the countries most influential leaders, such as Lisa Nichols, John Maxwell, Eric Thomas, Dr, Maricia Sherman, and sales strategist Erica Stepteau. No wonder why Larkeia Matthews is such a rising star in the empowerment and personal development industry, she has Tenaciously Overcome adversities untold, gleaned from and joining forces with powerful movers and shakers in the industry. She is a growing triple threat, Author, Transformational speaker, and Personal Power/Mindset coach. Larkeia specializes in the use of divine wisdom coupled with spiritual laws and strategies to retrain the brain, equip you to walk in your divinity and allow you take your power back.

Love King

Tarissa (Love) King is a writer, graphic designer, aspiring actress, and single mother of an amazingly beautiful talented 20-year-old daughter named Reyah King-Bledsoe. Love is a native of San Francisco California (The Bay Area) and has always been passionate about writing and creating stories. As a little girl she would write stories about her life growing up. Although these were kids books she kept to herself, they told the stories of real life events. Life has not been easy for Love and her experiences have helped her to be bold and brave and nonetheless loving towards people. Love has a creative soul that she is aspiring to develop into platforms that allow other women and children to be bold and brave to tell their stories through art and creativity. Love is original, authentic, dedicated, faithful, and powerful in Love!!

Love, Life, & Recklessness

Mz Mahoghany Reignz

I was born Stephanie Michelle Madden to my parents Debra Bradley and Larry Baker (R.I.P. 3-2-19) on the west side of Chicago, IL, we relocated to the south side where I grew up in the Altgeld Garden/Murray Homes. Growing up from the age of 9 to 23 in the projects taught me a lot. Life was rough but I always felt there was something greater for me. I was a single mother at the age of 17 and had 4 amazing, talented and beautiful children (Martise 25, Da'Keylah 22, Da'Kaylah 22 and Damecia Thomas 21). I left Chicago and everyone I knew in search of a better life for my children, so we moved to IA. In IA I went through a lot but gained even more. I am currently a featured food columnist for the local paper, I own and operate my own home based baking business and now a published author. I have 2 grandchildren (Prynce 3 and Pryncess 9 months) and one on the way (Baby N) in Jan 2020. I love expressive art in any form, but my favorites are Spoken Word and abstract art. Being a bit of a misfit myself I guess unique and eccentric people and things interest me. My passions are cooking, hospitality, writing and coloring in adult coloring books. Fun fact: I never prayed to God to be rich. I did pray to be impactful, productive and the first female host of The Family Feud.

Patti Denise Henry

A native of the Island of Trinidad & Tobago, Patti is internationally recognized as a Minister, Psalmist, Teacher, Hospice Chaplain, Family & Bereavement Counselor, Published Author and Prolific Speaker. She is also known as "A Prophetic Worshiper" as her sound in the earth impacts the heart and mind of all who come into contact with her ministry.

Patti Henry uses Biblical insight along with life experiences to help you to identify "The Holes in Your Soul" and provide the necessary tools to transform you into "Beautiful Souls".

She is the Founder & President of Patti Denise International Ministries, The Soul Coach and Sisters, Let's Keep Talking! Patti is humbled by the call that God has placed on her life and is very passionate about her purpose which is to multiply disciples for Christ and to function as a Soul Coach where she motivates others to live before they die. She is indeed a Servant Leader for such a time as this.

Srebrenica Lejla

Srebrenica Lejla is the Witty Werdsmith for Entrepreneurs. She works with entrepreneurs to achieve power in their brand messaging, get even clearer on their ideal client, while increasing profits through powerful, magnetic copy. Many businesses are sitting on gold mines and need a good translator to help amplify their message.

Serving as a Creative Mentor and Lifestyle Blogger, Lejla advocates for those to live their best creative life. In her supportive Facebook Group, The Lively Creatives, creative entrepreneurs are able to connect, share their challenges and wins. Through this, people in her community reap the benefits of powerful collaborations, for she believes there is much power in unity. Her first published book, Be Free, Live Creatively, was inspired by her Lifestyle Blog featured on www.thelivelycreative.com, focusing on mental health, life inspiration, and some of her crafty projects.

Aside from being a Lively Creative, Lejla has also excelled by becoming a two-time author in less than a year. As an MBA candidate, Srebrenica Lejla also enjoys crafty DIY projects, baking sweet treats, and exploring around the world.

You can learn more about Srebrenica Lejla and The Lively

Creative via:
Email: sb@thelivelycreative.com
www.thelivelycreative.com
FB: @thelivelycreativ
IG: @thelivelycreative_

Takima Howze

Takima Howze is a writer, speaker, and 2x self-published author. She is a millennial woman & mom who teaches women like herself on how to live The BRAVE Life™ by the power of their story. The BRAVE Life is a lifestyle brand that teaches millennial moms, coaches, and entrepreneurs how to be Bold, Resilient, Authentic, Victorious & Empowered in the midst frustration and fear by the power of faith. With an expertise in developing, creating, facilitating & teaching workshops for 10 years in the social service and education arenas Takima has taken her passion for writing, teaching and development to another level and is building a business that serves & helps others to share their BRAVE Stories.

She's A Creative Soul

Love, Life, & Recklessness

www.ingramcontent.com/pod-product-compliance
Lightning Source LLC
Chambersburg PA
CBHW071129090426
42736CB00012B/2062